THE CREATION

Elohim Creating Adam, by William Blake, courtesy of the Tate Gallery

THE CREATION

Winner of the 1993
Ohio State University Press / The Journal *Award in Poetry*

Bruce Beasley

OHIO STATE UNIVERSITY PRESS
Columbus

Copyright © 1994 by the Ohio State University Press.
All Rights Reserved

Library of Congress Cataloging-in-Publication Data

Beasley, Bruce, 1958–
    The creation / Bruce Beasley.
        p. cm.
        "Winner of the 1993 Ohio State University Press/*The Journal* award
in poetry."
        ISBN 0–8142–0623–9 (alk. paper). — ISBN 0–8142–0624–7 (pbk.
: alk. paper)
        I. Title.
PS3552.E1748C74   1994
811'.54—dc20   93-33496
                                                                        CIP

Text design by Victoria Althoff.
Type set in Goudy Old Style.
Printed by Cushing-Malloy, Inc., Ann Arbor, MI.

The paper in this book meets the guidelines for permanence and durability
of the Committee on Production Guidelines for Book Longevity of the
Council on Library Resources.

9 8 7 6 5 4 3 2 1

ACKNOWLEDGMENTS

I wish to acknowledge the magazines in which the following poems first appeared.

Agni ("Utter")

Antioch Review ("Zeta Hercules")

Denver Quarterly ("Ghost Elegy")

Hudson Review ("January Thaw," "Black Wednesday with Ashes," "Going Home to Georgia," "The Conceiving")

The Journal ("Advent: Snow Incantation," "Arcana Mundi," "Noli Me Tangere," "Longing," "Doxology")

Missouri Review ("The Fear of God")

New England Review ("The Instrument and Proper Corps of the Soule")

Ontario Review ("Sacrifice")

Paris Review ("Eve, Learning to Speak")

Poetry ("After an Adoration," "Consolation")

Poetry East ("Eternal Spring")

The Quarterly ("Wanting to Pray," "The Creation of Eve," "Sleeping in Santo Spirito," "Outside Paradise," "Sins")

Southern Review ("Noel," "Summer," "Tracing the Angel")

Southwest Review ("Vesper")

Yale Review ("Eurydice in Hades")

"Sleeping in Santo Spirito" also appeared in *Under 35: The New Generation of American Poets* (New York: Doubleday, 1989).

I wish also to thank Bill Wenthe, Dan Tobin, Bill Thompson, and Nancy Hurrelbrinck for their friendship and advice.

For Suzanne

No soul is at rest until it has despised as nothing all things which are created.

Julian of Norwich

The creation of man, whom God in His foreknowledge knew doomed to sin, was the awful index of God's omnipotence. For it would have been a thing of trifling and contemptible ease for Perfection to create mere perfection. To do so would, to speak truth, be not creation but extension. . . . The only way for God to create, truly create, man was to make him separate from God Himself, and to be separate from God is to be sinful. The creation of evil is therefore the index of God's glory and His power.

Robert Penn Warren

Contents

The Creation of Eve / 1
Eve, Learning to Speak / 4
The Fear of God / 7
Eurydice in Hades / 11
Summer / 13
The Instrument and Proper Corps of the Soule / 14
Tracing the Angel / 18
Sins / 21
Sacrifice / 24
Sleeping in Santo Spirito / 27
After an Adoration / 29
Eternal Spring / 31
Advent: Snow Incantation / 32
Arcana Mundi / 34
Consolation / 35
Ghost Elegy / 38
January Thaw / 41
Utter / 44
Zeta Hercules / 46
Noel / 48
Black Wednesday with Ashes / 50
Wanting to Pray / 52
Vesper / 53

Outside Paradise / 55
Noli Me Tangere / 56
Going Home to Georgia / 60
Longing / 63
Doxology / 66
The Conceiving / 70

The Creation of Eve

We lay a long time in the brine of my blood,

Father,
this other
   hacked from my flesh,

her side by my gashed side.
        Strangers—

How fitfully we slept like that, her hair
sponging the long cut
just under my heart . . .

We didn't speak, falling asleep, waking each other in starts—

both feverish. Once I dreamed
you were calling and calling
       and I
couldn't answer,
something caught deep in my throat—

It was days
before we could eat;
      I split
a lopsided fruit and squeezed

the juice from its hundred
scarlet seeds

into her mouth—

that's all she could take. So weak,
after being
            crushed into life in your hands . . .

I never asked
for another, didn't know
what to say to her, what to do—

the first three days we just
gazed, not talking,
over the east side of the hill
where you can see all four of the rivers
flowing
away from the garden
                        (where
do they go?)—I laid
my head in her lap and she
hummed,
and the sun

was dark by the slow-moving water;
we watched
three horned birds
                        I had not named
spiral above us,
black-winged and beaked, red-eyed—

My blood
still drained from the ragged cut, her skin
and mine both stained,
                        and our hair—

like the sky, a red we'd never seen—

and the birds
splayed their wings and tilted
above us in rings, circling
down to the bloody
mulch of fig leaves where we

kneeled . . .

My Father,
I never thought
                either of us
would heal—

Eve, Learning to Speak

A world already named, already
deposed
in the urge of his stressed
consonants, vowels
slack:
mood and *doom* and *sundown*, *logbridge*
and *pear*,
the gouge of the creek, hunched
leaves—

For days I called him *I*,

called the root in his fist
water, called what fire does
bathe—

He'd close me
for hours in the rivercliff
cave, as punishment,
to make me remember,
then he'd teach me its name: *alone.*

Alone,
I practiced the unnatural sounds,
touching my lips as he did,
feeling air
move through my throat, my chest,

letting it stay there.

Then sometimes the hush, the
thrill
of seeing things I hadn't learned to say,
things he hadn't claimed yet with his tongue:
once I woke, wet, hands muddy,
to something quick and burning
cutting through the trees.
And pieces of river
clinging to the spiderswings
between the crimped, rough applelimbs:

I would have kept that
as it was, tangible, alien,
let the memory
swell, unsayable—
and I stared at him,
refusing words,
when he came to rescue me
and teach me *rain* and *lightning*.

But some things
I kept as my own: the hurt
low in my body
he knew nothing of.
I came to like it. And my own
name for the land—not "Eden,"
not, even, a sound,
nothing any body could reproduce . . .

He wanted everything
common, reduced, so we could
exchange it, as though it were breath,
as though I still lay
deep in the bone and muscle of his side.

Sometimes I'd see myself
as I thought he must:
cut off, inviolable—
and I'd sit with him
and watch the high, cold grasses
all blowing one way.
I'd give in and let my strange
voice come.
And I'd feel the world diminishing, name by name,
as we talked through the long hours, and my new
life

hardened into form.

The Fear of God

Slashes of sleep & fitful dreaming,

& then it starts:
dust furious in sunlight, the Blue Ridge
quartered in windows,

God-vague & distant, smudged by sunrise.

⌘

A smother of bus smoke & low thunder,

& frozen shrubs
twist the recoiled crunch of their limbs.

The gingkos
peel, leprous behind their fence,
migrating
sparrows perched on the iron spires—

I can see
my breath marked on the damp air,

like the days scratched on a prisoner's wall.

Half the sky
scraped raw of its clouds, half-moon

bared—

Season of revelation, advent of love.

⌘

There's something
that watches us, & hoards its desire,
remote
from whatever it needs,

that waits
for all things to revert
to it, in death, & bides its time . . .

⌘

God is a circle,
Augustine says,
Whose center is everywhere,

whose circumference is nowhere . . .

⌘

It scares me, this restless
intelligence, desire
without form, without object, tonight,

clouds scavenging the moon, this yearning
I can't satisfy,
never pure, never sorrowful enough . . .

I want it
to leave me alone,
to atone
for my sins, one by one,
then forget

who I am, what I've done—

In a tangle
of branches, the low leaves
sheltering fruit,
I saw it once: a lit
face in a blur of apple leaves
as I spun past
on my grandfather's swing, arcing
over his great flowering yard. I thought I'd die,

thought I'd swing into the rough trunk
of that hundred-year-old tree,
his strong arms yanking the rope,
the heavens
just past the branches, & he pushed till I broke

free, sunspots in my eyes, clouds
forming & disassembling, something
secret calling me, hauling me on . . .

⌘

The heavens
can't be infinite, can't be full,
or there would be no darkness

in the night sky,
uncountable stars
from everywhere

would gorge us with their splendor—

You could never close your eyes against that light.

⌘

Suppose, at genesis, God
imagined every good the world
could hold,

9

then created them, one by one,
for us, as substitutes
for His love—

I envy della Robbia's
singing angels
their strange jubilation:
holding hands exulting,
blowing on their horns,
crowding over their hymnals,

beating out the time.

Eurydice in Hades

The stink of gingko pods, welter of sharp yellow leaves,
I remember

everything there. How smoke

wrapped and unwrapped the stripped trees,
mimicked, cloud by cloud, the whole sky,

torchlight on our faces, shadow and soot—

And pastures of sunflowers, swollen, grotesque, all bent
      toward the west
through the long-drawn summer afternoons,

and the slow grazing of horses hunched in the fields—

I remember
how the dark-blue berries of viburnum

burst and smeared on my feet in the rainy night,

and hailstones storming the meadows,
and the shock silver of olive leaves in the wind,

and the swollen purple puncture of the viper's bite on my
      heel—

Here the river arrives all day with its squalls,
barges scrape against docks

and the ferryman wards us back with his pole,

and the gnarling of the three dogs never subsides.
I spat out

the waters that would make me forget

when they captured me here
the first time,

remembering the smell

of mudbanks on a flooded river
above, the slap

of laundry against stone, and willows shining in the churning
water.

I know my own face still, though the mirrors are empty,
though the low murmur of prayers

to the death god and processions of candlelit shadows

tempt me to drink, just once,
from the shallow, tepid river and wash out

those fields of asters and poppies, gullies

rushing and overflowing with rain: all
the world I can't let go of, turning back

to witness again everything I've ever loved.

SUMMER

Between the lilac and pink dogwood, by the shrunken fig, a
   field of poison oak

spread, choked with scuppernong and the sharp
cracked shells of pecans.
I crouched there, in thunder, at sundown, searching

for rattlesnakes
or dead bodies, glass shards, hidden mouths of caves.
Whatever it took to disturb

the ordinary
sounds and smells of summer: the swamp-dark creek
at Moose Park,

horseshoes and Creedence Clearwater Revival
under the moon and floodlight,
my father, drunk at midnight,

watering the Cherokee rose
outside my window
for hours, whistling a sad, unnameable tune,

as I lay wide awake in the crackling
of mosquito lights, the transistor
pressed to my ear

buzzing all night its staticky claims of love.

THE INSTRUMENT AND PROPER CORPS OF THE SOULE

Yet is not this masse of flesh and visible structure the instrument and proper corps of the soule . . .

Sir Thomas Browne, Religio Medici

1

My mother brought me, from the butcher's,

a brain
lumped and blood-soaked in its plastic bag,

for my fifth-grade science project.
I held it to the light,

traced its cerebellum and medulla,
the lobes and hemispheres and fleshy folds

in which a cow's world resided:
grassy fields spiked with fences,

creeks wallowing in kudzu. On our kitchen table
the World Book lay open to a transparency

of the brain—a sheet you'd lay
over the drawing of a body

that filled in the skull
and marked each of the senses: arrows

to the seat of vision, of memory, of rage.

2

In 1634, Sir Thomas Browne
dissected the human

brain but found
no organ there

to contain the soul,
only layers of tissue, inscrutably folded,

nothing he could not find
as easily in the cranium of a beast.

3

Across the gray fat, the synaptic clefts—

the grooved, fissured
depths of his infolded brain—

a blood-clot grew through my father's
last years, the slow strokes

toward madness after years of liquor. Is that what gave
him such rage he'd hunt my mother

like a beast *Let go of me, children,
you're letting her get away . . .*

I hardly said a word to him for years
till he'd corner me and bellow

Goddammit are you mute,
and I'd turn away and shake my head.

4

Someone I love

has wept
for days, for no reason, the skewed

signals in her brain, glut

of dopamine at the cells
making her want nothing
but to die.

      —What
is the soul, that it
should surrender so abjectly
to the currents

and electrical misfirings of the flesh?

5

I don't know what the brain
can explain to us

when it burns
with all its world inside,

oxygen and blood gorging it,
clamoring to make sense of its signals.

Transmitters leaping through synapses
in the stalk

and hidden recesses of that flesh
determine too much of what we are:

my mother, in DTs, screaming
at my body flying over her bed

two months before vodka killed her.
It's what we can't see

that masters us, the mysteries
of blood and gods and brains

we're powerless against, no matter
how carefully we try to graph them,

name their parts, or hold them
carved and singled out for us into the light.

Tracing the Angel

In Bible School,
we traced the angel's
feather wing
on wax paper, joined it

to the drawn
figure of a boy.
With crayons in our fists
we made folds

in the robes, curls
in the hair. A cartoon
bubble like an air tank
to the mouth,

captions copied from Luke.
There was a prize
for the "most
realistic angel,"

for the graceful
juncture of shoulder
and wing, for making
believe a boy like us

could live
forever, floating

on angel wings,
and never get bored.

The stick-
figure angels
were the worst,
the sparrow

feather traced on the crossed
line of shoulder and arm,
the curved
face marking a smile.

Billy Miller—the boy
with the lopsided face
we called "Waterhead"—
spun himself around

and around
outside the Bible School,
singing *I see heaven,*
I see God;

his fat-
faced angel,
colored crimson,
took the prize.

God
watches the fall
of every sparrow,
letting them die

beside the roots
of the sycamore tree,
to be gathered for Vacation
Bible School, for boys

to crayon into wings
of cherubs, pressing
hard, making
visible the only ghosts

they're not yet scared to believe in.

SINS

On the first page of my Bible,
Adam and Eve
joined hands and skulked out of Paradise,
the serpent
flitting a red tongue, angels raising their whips.

The Bible was black, zipped up in leather.
In Sunday school, we'd smooth
down its gold cord tongue, marking
Genesis. God's words
rose from the page in red.

On blue
construction paper, in crayon,
Jesus
hung on the wall, His halo
smudged with glue.

My sins
were hammered to His cross,
they said;
His blood had washed my soul. Still,
they'd baptized us each with tapwater,

doused our first tufts of hair,
swaddled us musty at the altar,
while the congregation

moaned *Come home*
all ye sinners, come home . . .

⌘

The Sunday school smelled of mildew
and Clorox, paper cement.
Its closet held the grape juice
and crackers, Jesus'
blood and body; in church

the grownups would stain
their lips, clink
their cups on the brass tray.
The children's sermon taught us
how only

children could enter
the Kingdom of Heaven,
how Jonah
and Pinocchio both struggled
in the belly of the whale.

⌘

The ark was too
crowded. Lions and giraffes
hung over the sides of the balsawood kit.
The sheep
crushed Noah and his wife. The stuffed

sailboat leaked
when we set it adrift
in the Sunday school's kitchen sink . . .
So we learned how the world
had drowned

for its sins.
And one dove flew back
with a twig
in its mouth, meaning
forgiveness. That Sunday,

I noticed for the first time
how innocent
Jesus hung down
from the paned ceiling, his body
stained by the purple glass.

SACRIFICE

Sudden snowfall over flowering quince,

white rows of Bradford pears
turn, stripped of premature blooms in February wind.

Now the untimely spring retracts
its matted evidence: dying
honeysuckle snarled in forsythia; pollen
and pink, washed-out petals

blotting the hundreds of tiny puddles of snow.

⌘

Lush winter, the pink flush

of cherry trees in the last crack of light. Ash Wednesday,
a gray, drained afternoon
exhausted of all color
but this,
I lie on my bed and listen

to the Mighty Clouds of Joy
wailing *What a friend we have*
in Jesus, all
our sins and griefs to bear—

There's a neighbor sawing relentlessly
at the last

thin limb of his oak, while I watch,

through a film of pollen on the window,

lightning tear
at the blue, blurred hump of a distant mountain.

⌘

Today the world says enough, says it too well—
I want
to warn whatever issues

from its split, frozen side:

buds half-broken and burnt by frost,
gulled by whatever sense
binds them to this weather,
makes them yield, without knowing, to being born.

⌘

Sacrifice: I remember
the hush of prayers, in Florence,
old women

crawling on their knees toward a martyr

preserved in a glass coffin,
on the day of the Virgin's feast.
And the cemetery in Settignano, lit
by tiny torches on every grave,
blazing at sundown over wild-flowering hills.

I entered the basement where bones
of thousands of monks lay exposed
in Rome's
church of the Conception,

and walked through that damp, stone cellar

lined with sharded skulls,
skeletons hung in their brown monks' robes. Remembering
     they were ash
left tourists

stumbling, stunned and silent, back
to the rank July sun,
                    and the sidewalk bars
of American hotels, and ambulances'
wild honking in jammed circles of cars.

⌘

Now, in Charlottesville, I close my eyes,
listening—*Steal*
away to Jesus, I ain't got long to stay—

while the sacrifice of blooms

proceeds outside my window, cold
wind bearing upward
the withered, flesh-colored blossoms of flowering quince.

Sleeping in Santo Spirito

Shut out
of Masaccio's chapel where I'd tried
three times to see Eve and Adam

hunted by the angel, hiding
their genitals and eyes,
this afternoon I went instead

to sleep in the damp heat
of Santo Spirito. I watched
a priest in a black cassock,

swinging his silver censer, mount
the high altar to the Host
suspended among gold

to remake it into flesh.
Filthy, half-asleep, I thought
how the Gnostics wore black

to grieve
the soul's imprisonment in the flesh.
I watched him

consecrate and crack
the brittle tablet, dissolving it
bit by bit on his tongue, mumbling

Corpo di Cristo . . . Hunched
low in my seat at the dim

back of the altar, I fell

asleep as the congregation
rose in communion, their hymn
resounding foreign and hollow

across the vaulted glass.
My body was fouled
with sweat; I'd walked

miles to see the Expulsion, and stood
spent before the scaffolded chapel, its door
draped with a cartoon of the two

tormented figures. Aching
all over, I saw
that shut chapel again as I breathed

the holy smoke
of Santo Spirito, the votive
candles still burning behind my eyes. The black

back wings of the stone angel
smeared into sleep, with the wooden
donation boxes for the souls

of Purgatory, only
the faraway wailing of the Mass
holding me up.

I woke to a black-cloaked monk
staring me down, his harsh
eyes accusing me of sickness

or sacrilege: slouched
over a dim pew
carved with gnarled gargoyles, I was caught

half-asleep in the house of the Holy Ghost.

After an Adoration

They don't know what to do now they're here, leaning

on the rotted beam of a manger
bisected by light,

among oxen and asses, a carpenter's
tools, scrub

hills receding into blurred ruins.
Into each adoration, some peculiar

disillusion intrudes: always
someone in the crowd of pilgrims

averts his gaze from the Christ child
and glares accusingly outward

as though the arrival
had satisfied nothing. Only

the haloes redeem
the squalid scene: beasts'

breaths fuming in starlight,
barnfowl and peacocks flocked in the crossbeams.

One wise man's
mind has begun to go, and he stares

at some evil he believes

has followed him

the whole way, lodged now
in the shadowed rafters of this shed. Not

one of them could tell you what
all their longing

has accomplished: they're left
to stare into a wooden shack

where the cold
child whimpers and its mother

flails her arms in her sleep. After
an adoration, the shock

of how much remains
unrevealed; so awkwardly

the magi kneel
in the pawed dirt

littered with gold, beseeching the helpless savior.

ETERNAL SPRING

The morning you lost your child,
snow fell heavy over Atlanta,
blurring with rain
in the first week of April. The world
struck an unnatural pose: dogwoods
held their stiff, week-old
blooms against the wind; the azaleas'
pink flush felt out of season.
That morning I remembered Rodin's
Eternal Spring, how the naked
couple struggle to become one body,
how nearly they succeed,
rising starkly out of the stone,
the woman swept up on her knees,
the man's outsized hand
gathering in her breast
as his robe falls in waves away:
How sad
that sculpture seemed, that spring,
rejoicing
in the body, with your first
child miscarried, and the snow
falling over the pollen,
gathering flake by flake on the golden windows.

ADVENT: SNOW INCANTATION

Out of whose womb came the ice?
And the hoary frost of heaven, who hath
gendered it?

Job

Somewhere in the cold rot

of snowbanks
black with car exhaust, chokeberry
flattened and dragging
icicles down to steaming sewers,
cut ice
jangling dogwood limbs,

I mean to see
your spirit lay its shadow over the ice-light,

moon burnt-yellow and hard white over
hushed and rigid fields. Come
back to us, Father: this world

is your one sorrow, and it

will be rectified. Tonight, I know, you cross this field,
white on white,
through the seized puddles and swamps of December,

an ache of light
over the still pasture,
a headless snowman flapping its scarves
in unbroken wind,

while the roadside neon

delivers its message, word after word.

Can you hear
me, bodied as you are in the jagged chill, the freeze of slush
    and scattered berries?
Everything
rough and slick and shining
conceals you till I call
you back to this late fall, bedraggled magnolias
spotted with snow,
metallic scrape of shovels,
tinkling of mournful tin bells . . .

All fall I have dreamed
of lying down with you,
openmouthed in a downpour of snow,

eyelid and tongue covered, my white
breath buried,
and the heat of my flesh,

gone numb till I feel your chill
enter me at last: quick ash
falling over cold ash—

And then I wake and it's over, startled sunlight, sudden
    loosening of ice,
the faraway honking of cars
headed for work, frostburn
on my cheeks: the deep

recession into the ordinary

you order, hiding your face
inside the frozen drift of things, this shift of your whited earth.

ARCANA MUNDI

Everywhere doors stand open, everywhere
we dispose—with trouble—
of the familiar. A mockingbird
squawks and swoops to her nest in the tangled wild rose.
Strawberries hang, half-ripe, hollowed by birds.
Summer already withering. All day I've waited
in vain
for messages, accusations. Somewhere
the sea turns
its salt wounds to the sun. Somewhere saints fall
to their knees
on carved marble. Here, clouds
then stars
obscure the seven heavens.
The Boar flees through its haze, the Hunter moving low.
Cherry tree under their feet stripped of its fruit.
Look how the world whose mysteries
I meant
to reveal to you, thing by thing,
lowers its seven veils and lets us stare.

CONSOLATION

1

In February, the soul
always contracts, cracks
into ice, opaque and fouled
by tire ruts, matted straw, spilt oil—
contaminants
seized up and contained . . .

You can trace, in the frozen splashes,
layers of rain,
and the waste
that drifted inside—

Here in the split kingdom
of matter and spirit, the soul
doesn't recognize itself
in its natural emblems,
so I fill it in:
slash of ice
from the drainpipe, anything
straining forward
but congealed—

This winter, disconsolate, I hunger for nothing,

but the quarter-moon's

so bright you can see the rest of the globe
slightly outlined against the black,
the implied circle
closed.

2

In *Natural Theology*, William Paley
detected God's omnipotence
everywhere,
even in the providential design
of the stomach, the spuming of bile—

Everything surrendered God to him,
the story of resurrection
told and told again:
the eye *the best cure for atheism*;
membrania timpania—
microscopic bones of the ear—
revealing the intricate contrivance
of a God
bent on self-delivery
through the glorious works of His hands.

3

I loathe each day of my life;
I will take my complaint to God—

So Job laments, again, beginning
another Lent for me, in weary

February without mystery.
I walk the rough, dry woods

toward a river
crumbling the loamy banks of its gulch, ice-hatch

opening on to deep and glistening mud.
But we have to rid ourselves of the earth again,

of Job's sea *swaddled in shadows,*
of the leviathan and serpent and beasts God made,

for Meister Eckhart threatens
to be full of created things

is to be empty of God.
He consoles us with how good it is to suffer

in emptiness:
All sorrow comes from love and from holding dear.

This afternoon I tried to hold
nothing I could think of dear—but how quickly the world
    shrank from my touch,

and I loathed the burnt pastures bared to the sun,
and the useless

scrubs and flattened rocks and ice-flashing roofs of barns,
and all the divine effluvia I could see:

I gave it back
to God and lay myself, diminished and cold,

on the hard slab
by the half-frozen river, where the soul

stirred weakly in alien country, still hankering and unhealed.

GHOST ELEGY

Only the crimson ash tree
over your garden warns you
not to return:

the impermanence of everything
always oppressed you, the weight
of doing things all over again,

the waste
of fall and spring.
You wanted dying to be

completely different:
a distillation,
a sated hunger . . .

And now you've come halfway
home, after ten years gone, longing
for the black smoke in the night sky,

wanting to feel again
the mossy shells of old pecans,
the sunlight pooled on the cat's back.

⌘

There are times when you need
your death,

that quenched pain, the white
heat of bearing yourself
without any body:
feral now, and stray—

And there are times when you need
the cold
comfort of things, settled
in their dust, to know
the world could still be
ordinary, if
you wanted it to . . .

There are times
when you look into flame, with a sudden
shudder at seeing again,
and then
it thrills you, the way
the fire is like
you: nothing,
except for its burning,
its purging
of ash—

⌘

But grieving is never finished.
Tonight I watch fireflies wander
between the dogwood and the hedge,
lighting and vanishing and burrowing into the grass,
the sun
only an orange tracing of the Blue Ridge,
moths
thickening along the porch, light by light:

39

I listen
for the low strain of your voice,
trying to find me. What stays
gone from us never loved us, must have never hurt.

JANUARY THAW
(ELEGY FOR MY MOTHER)

Moonrise in full daylight by the weeping willow.
I ask you
what it is you've become, but you've got no voice now, no
    witness.
The hills bow
over the lake, over the ice-slicked fields
of mid-January, the day's last clouds
massed around the tips of the cherry trees, waiting for rain.

All day I've been trying to make
something of Meister Eckhart, reading
God is nearer to me
than I am to myself;
He is just as near to wood and stone,

but they do not know it . . .

I'm not sure
I know it, not sure
I can ever touch anything—no matter how close—
that has no body
to touch me back . . .

It's my thirtieth birthday,
Mama, and a thaw: the roots
of the cherry trees fisted
over the dwindled

41

fringes of snow that expose
the smothered grass. Almost
ten years to the day you died, the dead
grapevines trail into the rutted garden,
the gutters leaking a rust-colored slush. I wish I could show
    you
how the cherry trees
bulge from their coiled roots to the last

dripping, leaf-shaped huddles

of snow still trapped in their limbs.
I wish I could read you
this mystic
you'd understand now,
who would take God as he found Him,
in weeping as in joy.

Attached, as I am, to the things of this world,
I can no more know God
than the mouth knows a color, or the eye a taste,

says Eckhart. Then
what sense can I make
of you, in the dark
surrounding the hammock, only random
images for what you are: three stars
hammered into the night, the few ripped leaves,
slick mulch of snow-melt: what thaws
this birthday, this death
anniversary,
this mystic chanting in his unknowable tongue . . .

All this week of my birthday I've watched for you,

seen everything twice:
the streetlights half obscured by ice, half glaring,
frayed rose tendrils knotted on their metal trellis,

your grave glazed with snow . . .

But none of these things includes you.
You remember the world
imperfectly. In the split
ice of the lake our dog
almost drowned this afternoon, marooned
in his sudden pool, treading water,
waiting for me to wade in and break him free.
I can feel
you gazing at me, broken loose
ten years ago,
abandoned to your own soul . . .

Let go of me. The lullabies
and elegies chant you to sleep, Mama, wherever you are. To
    whatever
heaven where you'll wait for me, I commend you
with the words of this mystic
I long to believe—

the soul in which God
is to be born
must drop away from time, and time from her—

I close my eyes,
                I turn you away.

UTTER

If every utterance
               is set adrift,

floating without anchor from mind to mind

(whoever you are, believe me),
each word
heard, transformed, meaning

whatever we bend it into, I
can never reach you,
can't tell you this:

That there are streetlights
frozen in their own
glow, clouded
with ice, refracting
their light back inward,
a cold shine in the blown snow—

That there are creekbeds
crusted with blue
petrified wood, streaked
just beneath the waterline,
smoothed and colored by the water's unending flow.

That there are a hundred stars
in the Milky Way

for every man, woman, and child
on earth
to count them, to stake a claim—

That some nights, like this, before summer, the cherry trees
shiver in a hard wind, no moon,
no stars, an airplane
blinking like a lighthouse over the lawn,

the gods
      receding deeper and deeper into the withheld light.

Zeta Hercules

Thirty years ago, the year I was born,
Zeta Hercules

expelled its light. Across
hundreds of trillions of miles, I see it tonight:

the one star
fixed over the hammock and the scarred

trunk of the oak,
burning in the dim cluster where Hercules,

scorched
by his poisoned robe, kneels high in the night sky—

If it takes my birth star thirty years
to find me, God, how long must it take

my prayer to arrive where you
wait, more remote

even than Zeta Hercules,
more lost to the eye . . .

Years
after I die, will my prayer

suddenly pierce your sphere and move you,
will your answer

trail through the light-years of heaven
dividing us, the constellations

drawn clear in the cold sky, your face
etched at last out of the dark, the long

hem of your robe
grazing and grazing the hills by this house, still

hunting, after a hundred
years, for something

that once cried out,
something you needed to heal?

Noel

In December, the copper-
colored leaves
lie smeared along the sewer
grates, in the fourth
week of rain; holly
breaks through an iron
fence, its red
berries raw against the fog.
At the Monastery
of the Holy Ghost, peacocks
strut in their half-covered pen
this Christmas, pecking and dirty,
rattling the rain from their plumes.
A peacock
standing for everlasting life
perches over the manger
in Botticelli's *Adoration*; here,
their purple and green feathers
rise on thin wires, blue
tails the color of Mary's robes
dragging behind them in the mud.
Beside the lake the cherubs
carved for children's graves
are disfigured, the names
worn long ago from the stone.

They adorn
the abandoned cemetery
with the chipped strings of their harps.
Black cars
in funeral procession raise
a thick mist from the rain. They've come
to lay a body down, at Christmas,
in holy ground. The monks'
voices rise in chant from the cathedral,
confessing
the birth of a child without sin.
Red-winged
blackbirds descend, by the hundreds,
searching
for seed in the stubble grass.
They rise
all at once, their wingbeats
disturbing the prayer before
they vanish, dark and hungry, into the darker rain.

Black Wednesday with Ashes

I slept, & sleet
needled the windows, lightning & thunder & snow
& ambulance shriek
all woke me,

the telephone dead, stairs
slathered with ice,
the crunch of lost particulars,

white wiping out white—

This ennui of winter, this cursing it all.

⌘

There's no other world

this winter, no soul sets forth tonight:
I feel
the tangible world, the world of five senses,
enclose me, harden like impacted ice;
the smoke from a dozen houses
& all their ash
blacken the dark-gray sky, the trees

sharp-edged, tensed
without their leaves . . .

⌘

How perfect
to set the days of penitence
so deep in winter,
the black cowl,
the shrouded tabernacle,
sacred bones paraded through frozen streets:

what would we give
to have the spirit back
in black February, five o'clock dusk,

eighth day of rain,
withered stalks of dill . . .

⌘

The inner dark

brought outward, the cross
smudged over the brow, as we're
rechristened
in cinders, in smoldered

desire—

The shadows of hemlocks
stricken over smoothed snow.

Ice-rain all morning, wet thaw
& refreezing,
        layers of frozen melt:
The forty days
of repentence
come
so hard this winter, this cold

stripping the world
away, ache
by ache . . .

WANTING TO PRAY

Inside me a weak flame gutters.
I can feel
the blue of the bayed fire,
the dropped heat
of the tallow.
Then the frayed wick
dousing in its own wax.
Twilight
stains the oval
windows, the crucifix
and monstrance
swaddled in scarlet, not a sound
or a shadow
all through that black
chamber. Savior,
stranger, enter me again.

Vesper

One star
rises first from the dark of the cherry tree

I've picked from all day, the bucket
stained deep-pink below.

Hand over hand I've climbed
the thinnest branches,

past a bluejay hung half-decayed from its nest.
I didn't mean to watch the North Star

make its way after rain through the blue-green dusk,
hardly visible

in the night wind
through stormclouds and branches

distended with fruit.
I didn't mean to listen

to three dogs howling at each other across the sunset,
or look

down the barrel of a rotted limb
hollow and gummed with golden sap.

I wanted to let the summer
disappear into forgetfulness, a July rank with heat

drop from its own weight
and rot into the night wind, rain glazing the pink sphere,

black stem floating underneath:
I wanted to imagine this blooming yard

sharded with ice, an opaque round of it
shaped by the bird fountain

lopsided on its own melt, blistered
into pocks by the cold sun.

What I rose to instead was the harsh
particularity of summer, fruited and leaved,

starred and opening onto a lawn
I couldn't clarify

further: the whine
of yellowjackets in their sockets of earth,

dismembering moths, the thunder
of lawn mowers when the grass dries, whimper

of a golden retriever tethered
to a clothesline, cherries

trampolining the hammock, bees
swarming in their wake:

It takes
too much, I know, to fill me, to make

me desire things as they appear:
violent, redolent, summer-smeared.

OUTSIDE PARADISE

The scarlet berries and purple leaves of the pink dogwood in
    fall
surprise us. Across the porch,
the scrawny tree is fierce with color, impatient for spring.
Torn of their leaves, the cherry trees

scrape at the pink sky. In April they were laden,

skittering with bees, a thousand cherries borne on each limb.
It scared us, how we couldn't gather
half of them,
how they rotted on their stems, or split

and smeared deep red on the nubs of grass,

beyond our control, the way Paradise's
underbrush must have teemed, slithering
rubbery trunks, pond scum
breeding, sunflowers drooped into bloom, until Adam and Eve

would do anything it took to make it stop:

how they must
have flushed at the first
stiffening leaf, the wind
dragging the smell of the crumbling stems,

the richness of the fall instead of the rot.

Noli Me Tangere

1

Along the road to the Catacombs, I scaled a crumbling wall
where fig trees cracked the stone

with crabbed roots, dropping fruit
that smeared under Fiats and Vespas. Thunderheads

swaddled the umbrella pines, begonias
huddled around the doorway

of the oil-lit chambers of the dead.
Smolder of incense above the blackened

and fragmented wing of an angel.
A sullen priest

led us through saved
tunnels an earthquake unearthed:

crosses and fish-shaped graffiti,
the names

of apostles chipped in the damp stone,
skulls propped in their beds.

A fresco of Paradise, dim rose
and lamb and dove, survived

above the empty urns, in a russet
flare of the swinging oil lamp

past peacocks in acanthus and lotus,
the prayers of African pilgrims

scratched into the wall
begging for intercession

for the souls of the holy dead.
The leviathan

vomited Jonah out on the sea,
out on the hallway,

his face worn forever into the colorless stone.
Bone by bone,

the saints moldered beyond these hollows,
recoiled from the dark cavern

and turned bodiless back to the light.

2

In the story of the cursed fig tree,
there's no ripeness

that can satisfy a god's hunger,
only a barrenness like that of the body

when it craves and cannot have:
Is it curses

the flesh needs, holding what's natural back?
Soon Christ would be gone from nature,

from anything we could touch;
the hunched, overgrown fig trees

bearing their bruised summer load,
figs split, their folds

riddled by swarms of green flies,
carnal and splattered

over the stone road, inedible, crushed in their skin.

3

In the sacristy of Santa Croce,
Korean pilgrims chant Latin hymns

on their knees before St. Thomas' finger
held in jeweled glass.

It was an act
of faith, the apostle's

insistence on that flesh,
the bruised skin torn from the rib cage,

the stabwound
swollen, tender, unhealed by rebirth.

I can't doubt anymore these saved
fragments of the body, whose glass

reflects to me my own worn face,
and I can't bow

before the decayed finger
that stanched the blood of a god. Thunder

cracks at the church when the hymn ends, hailstones
pounding the stone portico,

and we huddle in shelter, humming
How Great Thou Art as the storm

racks the streets of Rome,
a priest sweeping the rainwater back.

The Etruscans
believed the gods were furious

to communicate with us, that each
of the hundred sounds of thunder formed a word

we had to translate, that clouds
clashed only so we would have thunder

and lightning and voices of gods,
bodiless, working the natural world

to touch us and make us worship
the way only we

can, in tenderness and dread.

GOING HOME TO GEORGIA

Beyond the pawn shops and tattoo parlors and Tofu House
of Atlanta, the highway drones
out to the squat, clipped peach trees
in pink and green flower
and the roadside doublewide
V.I.P. Massage Parlor
("Truckers Welcome")
and the purple

quilts of Leonardo's *Last Supper*
flapping in the March wind, by the gargoyles
and lawn gnomes
and tin-roofed shacks,
and crosses scrawled with warnings of hellfire,
and buzzards

wheeling low. I remember, suddenly, Orvieto—
how, in Signorelli's fresco
of the torments of the damned,
the noose
by which a devil strangles a young woman
has disappeared, worn down
by centuries on the church wall. And he yanks,

still, at the nothing between them,
his green foot pressed to her temple,

while the green- and pink-winged angels

stand arrogant over the scene, beating back
the rising damned,
barely glancing at the horrors below.

There's enough we can see
to choke us
in the crumbling chimneys and steeples
in the half-rain, half-sun
of this late afternoon,
the Buford Highway Body Shop's
billboard: "Jesus Christ
is the way, truth, and light. Free

estimates . . . "

—I've come back to Macon for the first time
in years, the Ocmulgee River's
old smell of thick mud and stagnating
water and honeysuckle
blent
through what's left of Baconsfield Park.
Willed
by a Confederate general "for the enjoyment
of white women and children,"
it's sold now

by Supreme Court order and sporting
McDonald's and condos surrounding
the swampy,
magnolia-shadowed pond

where I, a white child, gathered
salamanders
with my father

from the crevices of mossy rocks
twenty-six years ago.

By the river the graves of my parents
lie abandoned, side by side,
with five years separating their last
miserable days,
the obscure torments of the drunk
that drove them both to want to die, to lie
down here before their time
and let
the world and its cravings fall away.
I've come back with what I've been able
to shore against their dread,
what things might suffice to heal
this world
without losing it: rainy
sunlight over Rose Hill, miles
of pool halls and wrecked Plymouths, mounds
of hubcaps and inner tubes, wild
iris and cabbage palm and stakes of crosses—for the first
time since they died I can breathe
the sweet, soiled air
of this swampy burying ground
again and answer them both

it's enough, and enough, the stuff of this world.

LONGING

On Easter morning I'm reading
a Gnostic account of Creation: how Wisdom
longed to know her father, the source of all things, but found
    Him
impossibly remote, unfathomable even to her;
to salvage her failure, she crafted
the universe
out of the four sorrows of her longing:
grief into air, fear into water,
shock become earth,
                ignorance fire.

I like to think
what surrounds us this damp morning
is all a creation
of what we can't know,

that some longing inheres
in these shoots
of tulips and daylilies bent under rain,

mudwash
in the birdbath, cherryblooms drifting through the grief of
    the air.

I like to believe there's a failing

our taste and smell and touch
compensate for, an absence
I'm filling back in
when I breathe the wet loam, stinkweed and chicory.
When I crush this soaked forsythia
in my fist, the fear
of what's unknowable

dries in the friction of flesh against flesh.

⌘

Each Easter we try to surrender
to mystery: what rises
out of the knowable world.
At Sunrise Service in Macon, once,
on a hill hunched over downtown,
in the shadow of massive crosses,

a PA system
tuned to the wrong station
greeted the Resurrection at dawn,
blasting *The Boogie-Woogie Bugle Boy of Company B*.

And the worshippers loved it: shrieks
of laughter in the half-light,
high heels and painted nails
tapping out its fast beat.

        —We bleed
the world of mystery, settle
among its elements instead:
sunrise burning in ignorance over the riverbed,

pink dogwood's frayed petals
waving just behind the cross,

the shock
of earth always pulling us down,
lilac and camellia curled in the dirt,
ourselves and everything we see
pieced
together from a longing
that can never be quenched.

Doxology

Let me praise you, God of salve and hurt,
begetter
of all things
marred
and mercy ridden—

          This
sprout of beggarweed, these lilac stalks
need
say nothing: look how their whole
form
extols you, scrub and vine. And even
the slackwater
odor
of full gullies in drifts of sludge
attests to you—

But I, who live
on words, can never
praise you enough:

what use is language—there's nothing
the heavens can't say
in their own praise, and haven't
uttered
already in shudders

of creation
more firm than words . . .

I have dreaded, secretly, your earth,
its capacity to hurt
whoever loves it
too much: Flock
of blackbirds over dull neon
in Thanksgiving's
rainy dusk, rush
of wind through bare sweet
cherry, swelter of squirrels:

so little

abides,
so much recalls our turning
back toward you,
from whom all blessings flow
endlessly away:

magnificats
of dilapidated
dogwoods, hallelujahs in the western
burn,
lauds of what can't stay
. unspeakable . . .

My God, this world has ached
with secret
adoration: let language
cohere until I can utter it:

let what I call out for
come for me
sometimes,
and what I mean

and what it means for me

touch—

⌘

This is the found world, desacralized,

where the crooked dogwood
kneels in November quarter-sun
over dead tufts of dianthus, blue-moon, and phlox, gusts
expired
with side-driven rain.

This is the world I grieve
without having lost it, the material
of your withdrawal
from us
that bears, nonetheless, a witness:
hierophanous
squalls in thunder, immeasurable want—

Only we have the soul
to reject you: scraped hills
abound in the form of your glory,
scrunched
waves over driftwood in bayshores
spume into landspits, oblivious;

and only we have the intelligence
to expose you
in the workings of what you've made:
not one spasm or rift of earth—
susurrus, then silence, of rain—
fails to report you
to whatever can listen
with astoundment enough.

—Listen, my God, for what
worship
I can utter in language, fallen
medium:
heal me so that I can say
only the word
that will mirror you, at least,
in one piece

of all your insensible world.

THE CONCEIVING

1

What is this weariness
with breath after breath after breath,

this turning-inward
to escape from smaller and smaller

talk? I have always wanted to be
anonymous, unbidden into speech,

withdrawn
into what remnant of the spirit's

left in me,
and there I find you,

uncreated, in that poverty of the senses
where you stay,

prefœtal and invisible and blind.
If I make us a haven

here inside,
hypostasis of father and child,

not physical yet, not real,
will you let me lead you back

to earth someday, will you forgive
what avarice makes us make you

come alive? This transubstantiation
would give you years

of pleasure intense and always receding, a world
so glutted with things I sometimes make my way

out of it awhile
to rest in your stripped landscape; going out,

I cut a swath
from here to there, a clearing

by which someday you'll find your own way in.

2

Here at the Cinque Terre—
the five earths—
we wait for you
in raw, unmediated places, an earth
almost too physical to endure:
surfspume into algae-colored grottoes of cloven stone,
octopus-tendrilled
cactuses crawling off seacliffs,
here where the soul's
impossible to tell
from the objects of its appetite:
burnt crusts of bread, strips
of black-roasted red peppers, oozing their oil:

five earths, five senses, what veils and seals to tear—

3

Look at the gulls stunned over downbent sea-pines,
and the schooners anchored in the noon-still of the bay,

and the lighthouse waiting, witholding
its timed
shocks—

It's a world
with a stasis of its own,
and flux as well: smell,
all at once, these rosemary sprigs
on turning skewers of chicken,
and tufts of honeysuckle,
and the salt
sea—

Then beg creation to admit you,
the way roots
that have cracked a stone wall
grow thick, sealing the fissure . . .

4

Untethered one, if you dare
enter this place of appetite
and satiation—
the slag and dross of hungers and of love—
with nothing but sleep and prayer
to take you back,

how we'll hold you,

and recite you the new world's things:
sienna, magenta, ivory,
woodgrain and grain of stone,
shrunk soap,
heaped peaches, exultation
of bells—

Such profusion

you'll watch recede from you,
richer and more splendid as it goes,
hour after hour,

sandspit and grave.

5

This life of the body, this ceaseless prayer,

how can I tell it to you?
It costs distance, and diminishment,

wave after wave raised from a lost disturbance,
some mid-ocean squall

that gave them birth.
But see with what ravishment

and splendor they arrive,
here where slate's

layered over limestone, seagrass, and slime,
where the Gulf

of Paradise floods the land's hollows.
It's labor

and a kind of worship, to let creation
enter through the senses,

in all its defective
splurge: poppies on mulepaths,

teal glut of the surf
the instant before it breaks: come bear

witness with us, child, among
the things that come and overwhelm us and vanish again.

The Ohio State University Press / *The Journal*
Award in Poetry
DAVID CITINO, Poetry Editor

1992	Dionisio D. Martínez	*History as a Second Language*
1991	Teresa Cader	*Guests*
1990	Mary Cross	*Rooms, Which Were People*
1989	Albert Goldbarth	*Popular Culture*
1988	Sue Owen	*The Book of Winter*
1987	Robert Cording	*Life-list*

The George Elliston Poetry Prize

1987	Walter McDonald	*The Flying Dutchman*
1986	David Weiss	*The Fourth Part of the World*
1985	David Bergman	*Cracking the Code*